An Educational

Read and Color

Book of

PLAINS INDIANS

EDITOR
Linda Spizzirri

COPY REFERENCE
Department of
the Interior

ILLUSTRATION
Peter M. Spizzirri

COVER ART
Peter M. Spizzirri

CONTENTS

TRIBE NAME: DAKOTA (Sioux)

LANGUAGE: SIOUAN

WHERE THEY LIVED: MINNESOTA AND WESTWARD

KIND OF HOUSE: TEPEE

WHAT THEY ATE: BUFFALO, GAME, FISH AND
FOREST   FOREST PRODUCTS

INTERESTING FACTS:

The Sioux have long been identified as the great Plains Indian culture. They were originally woodland Indians whose homeland was just west of the Great Lakes. Famed for their resistance to the white man and for their dominant role in the plains wars, the Sioux became the model for Indians in television, movies and novels. Names of famous Sioux leaders, such as Sitting Bull and Crazy Horse have become household words. The Sioux were of a numerically large tribal group, with thousands of warriors. They were the finest and most feared horsemen of the Great Northern Plains.

SIOUX WAR CHIEF →
WITH BATTLE STANDARD

TRIBE NAME: KIOWA

LANGUAGE: KIOWAN

WHERE THEY LIVED: SOUTH DAKOTA

KIND OF HOUSE: TEPEE

WHAT THEY ATE: BUFFALO, HUNTED GAME, PLAINS
                     FOOD PRODUCTS

INTERESTING FACTS:

The original homeland of the Kiowas was western Montana. The Kiowas left this area, because of the tribal disputes over hunting spoils, and settled in the Black Hills of South Dakota. The Kiowas were only small game hunters until they formed an alliance with the Crow Indians. The Kiowas then became buffalo hunters with large herds of horses. They became a typical Plains Indian tribe, using the buffalo skin tepee, medicine bundles, and having a big annual summer "Sun Dance." The "Koitsenko" was the Kiowan term for their warriors soldier society.

BUFFALO HUNT →

TRIBE NAME: ARAPAHO

LANGUAGE: ALGONQUIAN

WHERE THEY LIVED: COLORADO AND WYOMING

KIND OF HOUSE: TEPEE

WHAT THEY ATE: BUFFALO AND HUNTED GAME

INTERESTING FACTS:

Once sedentary farmers, the Arapahos are believed to have traveled from the Red River in Minnesota to the headwaters of the Missouri River, crossing into the plains. The Arapahos separated as they moved into the plains and became semi-nomadic. Like the other Plains Indians, Arapaho life centered around the search for the buffalo. The tribal male was ceremonious and full of valor. Beadwork ceremonially adorned their robes and lodges. The eight secret societies and the annual "Sun Dance" played an important part in lives. The most important sacred object was the Flat Pipe.

THE GHOST DANCE →

Arapaho

TRIBE NAME: OSAGE

LANGUAGE: SIOUAN

WHERE THEY LIVED: MISSOURI AND KANSAS

KIND OF HOUSE: OVAL OR RECTANGULAR HOUSES
                    COVERED WITH SKINS

WHAT THEY ATE: BUFFALO AND OTHER GAME

INTERESTING FACTS:

The Osage built oval or rectangular houses that had straight walls and curved roofs, which they covered with mats or skins. These buildings ranged in size from 30 to 100 feet in length, 15 to 20 feet in width and averaged 10 feet in height. There is a suggestion here of the Iroquoian longhouse, but as yet, there is no knowledge of any contact between the two peoples.
In 1673, the great French explorer Marquette located these people on the Osage River.

COURTSHIP →

TRIBE NAME: BLACKFEET

LANGUAGE: ALGONQUIAN

WHERE THEY LIVED: MONTANA

KIND OF HOUSE: TEPEE

WHAT THEY ATE: BUFFALO AND GAME

INTERESTING FACTS:

The Blackfeet were among the first of the Indian groups to leave the forests of the northeast for the northwestern plains. Through trade, the Blackfeet had attained horses and weapons, making them the strongest military power on the northwest plains. The semi-nomadic culture of the Blackfeet was the same as the plains tribes, they followed the buffalo. They were always famous horsemen and hunters.

SCOUTING PARTY →

Black Feet

TRIBE NAME: CHEYENNE

LANGUAGE: ALGONQUIAN

WHERE THEY LIVED: NORTH AND SOUTH
                     DAKOTA

KIND OF HOUSE: TEPEE

WHAT THEY ATE: BUFFALO AND GAME

INTERESTING FACTS:

The Cheyenne were originally natives of the Minnesota woodlands. They moved further west to the Black Hills of South Dakota, where Lewis and Clark found them in 1804. From there, they were pushed southwest into the Great Plains by the Sioux Indians. They gradually stopped harvesting crops, such as corn, when they started this southwest movement. By the time they were forced to the plains, the Cheyenne were living in skin tepees and had become buffalo hunters. The Cheyenne were traditionally proud and brave. The men were known for their fine strong physiques and the women were expected to be virtuous.

The most famous of the Cheyenne tribal societies was the "Dog Soldiers." Many of its members fought in the Battle of Little Big Horn against General George Armstrong Custer and his "Pony Soldiers".

SMOKING THE CALUMET →

Cheyenne

13

TRIBE NAME: MANDAN

LANGUAGE: SIOUAN

WHERE THEY LIVED: NORTH DAKOTA

KIND OF HOUSE: EARTH LODGE

WHAT THEY ATE: BUFFALO, GAME AND HARVESTED
                   CROPS

INTERESTING FACTS:

The Mandans were a large and powerful tribe of the plains. The family lived in earth lodges that were so large, the warriors favorite horses could also be stabled in the lodge. The family baskets, dance costumes, spears and skins filled the lodge. The framework of the lodge was made of wooden poles and from the poles hung the assorted gear that the family used (shields, boat paddles, moccasins, etc.).

BUFFALO DANCE →

15

Mandan

TRIBE NAME: PAWNEE

LANGUAGE: CADDOAN

WHERE THEY LIVED: NEBRASKA AND KANSAS

KIND OF HOUSE: EARTH LODGE

WHAT THEY ATE: BUFFALO, GAME AND HARVESTED
                     CROPS

INTERESTING FACTS:

For half of the year, the Pawnee tribe left their permanent earth lodge villages on the Platte River for the southwest plains, to hunt for the buffalo. When they returned to their villages in the fall, they harvested their crops, which they had planted before leaving on the buffalo hunt. After the crops were harvested, the Pawnee spent the rest of the fall and winter in hunting and raiding parties. The raiding parties were mainly horse stealing expeditions that took the Pawnee as far south as New Mexico. The principle enemies of the Pawnee were the Sioux, Cheyenne, Kiowa and Commanche.

PAWNEE MEET CHEYENNE →

Pawnee

TRIBE NAME: CADDO

LANGUAGE: CADDOAN

WHERE THEY LIVED: ARKANSAS, TEXAS, OKLAHOMA

KIND OF HOUSE: SQUARE HOUSE WITH GRASS ROOF   AND CLAY WALLS

WHAT THEY ATE: GAME, CORN AND OTHER CROPS THEY GREW

INTERESTING FACTS:

Archaeological research shows the Caddo people to be of ancient heritage. The daily life of the tribe was regulated by their religion and by astronomical observations. Their friendly presence was very important to the early French and Spanish colonials.

The Caddo had an advanced knowledge of farming. The tribe lived on scattered farmsteads with the temple mounds as a ceremonial and social center for the tribe. The farm work was done by the women and provided the major source of their food supply. Men supplemented the food supply by hunting.

CORN DANCE →

TRIBE NAME:	HIDATSA
LANGUAGE:	SIOUAN
WHERE THEY LIVED:	NORTH DAKOTA
KIND OF HOUSE:	EARTH LODGE
WHAT THEY ATE:	BUFFALO, GAME, FISH, AND CROPS THEY FARMED

INTERESTING FACTS:

In the 17th century, raiding parties of Cree and Ojibwa warriors, armed with white man's guns, forced the Hidatsa from their homeland onto the plains. The Hidatsa settled on the Big Bend of the Missouri River. The buffalo hunt soon assumed a role of major importance in their lives. Previously, the Hidatsa left their villages for only a few weeks out of each year, but on the plains, they were gone from their lodges most of the time. They returned home only for planting, harvesting and for the winter months. Like all tribes of the plains, they followed the nomadic life of the buffalo. The Mandan and Hidatsa were the only two tribes to have a "White Buffalo Society" for women only. The women of the society would dance "to lure the Buffalo."

WOMEN OF THE WHITE BUFFALO SOCIETY →
DANCING "TO LURE THE BUFFALO" →

Hidatsa

TRIBE NAME: CROW

LANGUAGE: SIOUAN

WHERE THEY LIVED: MONTANA AND WYOMING

KIND OF HOUSE: TEPEE

WHAT THEY ATE: BUFFALO, GAME, FISH AND HARVESTED CROPS

INTERESTING FACTS:

The Crow were among the most notable horsemen of the northern plains. Only the Comanche owned as many horses. The Crow were a tall and handsome people. The tribeswomen had such superior skill at tanning and embroidery, they decorated their saddles, bridles, collars, blankets and clothing. They so richly ornamented their possessions with such skill and beauty that their handwork was unrivaled on the plains.

THE BUFFALO ARE HERE →

Crow

23

TRIBE NAME: COMANCHE

LANGUAGE: UTO-AZTECAN

WHERE THEY LIVED: TEXAS AND OKLAHOMA

KIND OF HOUSE: TEPEE

WHAT THEY ATE: BUFFALO, AND GAME, PLUS FOOD
                      PRODUCTS THAT WERE AVAILABLE
                      ON THE PLAINS

INTERESTING FACTS:

The Comanche were one of the southern tribes of the Shoshonean stock and the only ones to live entirely on the plains. Being nomadic buffalo hunters, the Comanche made little agricultural use of the land. Known as the finest horsemen of the Plains, they had a reputation for courage and considered themselves superior to neighboring tribes.
The Comanches resented the Texans for taking their best hunting grounds from them. They waged a relentless war against them for 40 years, until the signing of the Medicine Lodge Treaty in 1867.

COMANCHE BOWMAN →

Comanche

TRIBE NAME: SHOSHONE

LANGUAGE: UTO-AZTECAN

WHERE THEY LIVED: WYOMING AND MONTANA

KIND OF HOUSE: TEPEE

WHAT THEY ATE: BUFFALO, GAME AND PLAINS
                      FOOD PRODUCTS

INTERESTING FACTS:

The northern bands of Shoshone were found by Lewis and Clark in 1805, on the headwaters of the Missouri River in western Montana. They had been driven from the plains by the hostile Atsina and Siksika tribes who possessed firearms from the white man. After fleeing the plains, the Shoshone were able to fight and hold their new territories against the weaker western tribes.

SHOSHONE VILLAGE →

Shoshone

27

TRIBE NAME: WICHITA

LANGUAGE: CADDOAN

WHERE THEY LIVED: KANSAS AND OKLAHOMA

KIND OF HOUSE: ROUND GRASS STRUCTURE

WHAT THEY ATE: GAME FOOD, FISH AND CROPS
                   THEY FARMED

INTERESTING FACTS:

The Wichita had a very orderly life. The father to son heredity pattern was well established. The women of the tribe did the farming and supplied the majority of food for the family. The men added to the food supply by hunting. Religion and astronomy, which they learned from their Caddo ancestors, played an important part in the daily lives of the Wichita Indians. The Wichita lived on small farmsteads, like the Caddo. The farmsteads were near temple mounds that were used as social, cultural and religious centers.

WICHITA VILLAGE →

TRIBE NAME: OMAHA

LANGUAGE: SIOUAN

WHERE THEY LIVED: IOWA, SOUTH DAKOTA, NEBRASKA

KIND OF HOUSE: TEPEE

WHAT THEY ATE: BUFFALO, GAME AND HARVESTED CROPS

INTERESTING FACTS:

The Iroquois drove the Omaha from the Ohio River Valley onto the plains. These new immigrants to the plains quickly took advantage of the plains buffalo as a source of meat supply. The buffalo hunt became the main source of food supply, replacing village farming and food gathering searches. The Omahas had many social societies, some secret and some open. The "Thunder Society," for example, was responsible to act as custodian of the two sacred pipes. The "Bear Dreamers" was a secret society that practiced sleight of hand tricks and such things as swallowing long sticks. The "Buffalo Dreamers" excelled in treating wounds. Members of the military societies were first in war, formed raiding parties, commanded during the tribal hunt, guarded the camps, and sponsored feasts, games and dances. Their most important function was that of historian and teacher, its members passed on the tribal lore and knowledge.

VISITING NEIGHBORS →

AWARD WINNERS
SPIZZIRRI PUBLISHING, INC
100 Best Childrens Products Award COLOR BOOK/CASSETTES

Factual information, dramatic narration, sound effects and music make these cassettes and books a special learning experience every child will remember with pleasure.

THREE CASSETTE LIBRARY ALBUM
YOUR CHOICE OF 3 STORY CASSETTES AND BOOKS IN A PLASTIC STORAGE CASE
SPI 222-9

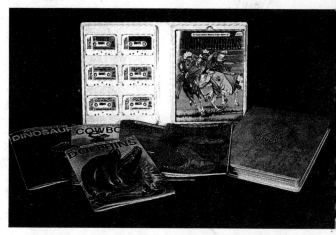

Dr. Toy
100 BEST
CHILDREN'S
PRODUCTS
1995

INDIVIDUAL BOOK AND CASSETTE PACKAGE

SIX CASSETTE LIBRARY ALBUM
YOUR CHOICE OF 6 STORY CASSETTES AND BOOKS IN A PLASTIC STORAGE CASE
SPI 169-9

INDIVIDUALLY BOXED CASSETTES
All cassettes are in reusable plastic cases.
SPI 224-5

48 DIFFERENT TITLES TO CHOOSE FROM
ALL INDIVIDUAL CASSETTE AND BOOK PACKAGES

SPI 109-5 AIRCRAFT	SPI 152-4 COWBOYS	SPI 091-9 NORTHWEST INDIANS	SPI 101-X REPTILES
SPI 096-X ANIMAL ALPHABET	SPI 107-9 DEEP-SEA FISH	SPI 149-4 PACIFIC FISH	SPI 114-1 ROCKETS
SPI 104-4 ANIMAL GIANTS	SPI 082-X DINOSAURS	SPI 147-8 PENGUINS	SPI 105-2 SHARKS
SPI 148-6 ATLANTIC FISH	SPI 161-3 DOGS	SPI 151-6 PIONEERS	SPI 156-7 SHIPS
SPI 159-1 BIRDS	SPI 095-1 DOLLS	SPI 089-7 PLAINS INDIANS	SPI 092-7 SOUTHEAST INDIANS
SPI 094-3 CALIFORNIA INDIANS	SPI 108-7 DOLPHINS	SPI 112-5 PLANETS	SPI 093-5 SOUTHWEST INDIANS
SPI 160-5 CATS	SPI 103-6 ENDANG'D SPECIES	SPI 158-3 POISONOUS SNAKES	SPI 110-9 SPACE CRAFT
SPI 102-8 CATS OF THE WILD	SPI 153-2 ESKIMOS	SPI 084-6 PREHIST. BIRD	SPI 111-7 SPACE EXPLORERS
SPI 085-4 CAVEMAN	SPI 154-0 FARM ANIMALS	SPI 086-2 PREHIST. FISH	SPI 098-6 STATE BIRDS
SPI 150-8 COLONIES	SPI 162-1 HORSES	SPI 087-0 PREH. MAMMALS	SPI 163-X STATE FLOWERS
SPI 113-3 COMETS	SPI 100-1 MAMMALS	SPI 083-8 PREHIST. SEA LIFE	SPI 155-9 TRANSPORTATION
SPI 097-8 Count/Color DINOSAURS	SPI 090-0 NORTHEAST INDIANS	SPI 157-5 PRIMATES	SPI 106-0 WHALES

SPI 480-9 48 CASSETTE AND BOOK ASSORTMENT